W9-BZB-138

RACE IN
AMERICA

ROOTS OF
RACISM

BY KELLY BAKSHI, MS ED

CONTENT CONSULTANT
Dr. Eileen O'Brien
Associate Professor of Sociology
Associate Chair, Department of Social Sciences
Saint Leo University, Virginia Campus

Essential Library

An Imprint of Abdo Publishing | abdopublishing.com

ABDOPUBLISHING.COM

Printed in the United States of America, North Mankato, Minnesota
042017
092017

THIS BOOK CONTAINS
RECYCLED MATERIALS

Interior Photos: ullstein bild/Getty Images, 4–5; Popperfoto/Getty Images, 7; Carl Iwasaki/The LIFE Images Collection/Getty Images, 11; Arno Massee/Science Source, 13; Stefano Bianchetti/Corbis Historical/Getty Images, 16–17; Mansell/The LIFE Picture Collection/Getty Images, 20; Bettmann/Getty Images, 21; Sean Pavone/Shutterstock Images, 24; PHAS/Universal Image Group/Getty Images, 27; Universal History Archive/Universal Images Group/Getty Images, 28–29, 31; Paul D. Stewart/Science Source, 36–37, 41; Wellcome Library/London/Johann Friedrich Blumenbach/Mezzotint by F. E. Haid, 39; Shutterstock Images, 43; Education Images/Universal Images Group/Getty Images, 44–45; Georgios Art/iStockphoto, 48; North Wind Picture Archives, 50–51, 56, 58, 83; MPI/Archive Photos/Getty Images, 60–61; iStockphoto, 63, 93, 96; John N. Choate/MPI/Archive Photos/Getty Images, 66; Picture History/Newscom, 68; Augustus F. Sherman/William Williams/Manuscripts and Archives Division/New York Public Library, 70–71; FPG/Archive Photos/Getty Images, 73; Everett Historical/Shutterstock Images, 76–77; Fabina Sbina/Hugh Zareasky/Getty Images News/Getty Images, 80–81; Clem Albers/War Relocation Authority/Department of the Interior/National Archives, 85; Kena Betancur/AFP/Getty Images, 89

Editor: Arnold Ringstad
Series Designer: Maggie Villaume

PUBLISHER'S CATALOGING-IN-PUBLICATION DATA

Names: Bakshi, Kelly, author.
Title: Roots of racism / by Kelly Bakshi, MS Ed.
Description: Minneapolis, MN : Abdo Publishing, 2018. | Series: Race in America |
    Includes bibliographical references and index.
Identifiers: LCCN 2016962261 | ISBN 9781532110375 (lib. bdg.) |
    ISBN 9781680788228 (ebook)
Subjects: LCSH: Race--Juvenile literature. | Racism--Juvenile literature. | Prejudices--Juvenile literature. |Minorities--Juvenile literature.
Classification: DDC 305--dc23
LC record available at http://lccn.loc.gov/2016962261

CONTENTS

JESSE OWENS BUSTS RECORDS AND MYTHS

African American athlete Jesse Owens took his place at the starting line for the long jump event. The German crowd for the 1936 Berlin Olympics filled the arena with the sound of their cheers. Looming around the city's Olympic Stadium were enormous red-and-black Nazi flags. Over the previous decade they had come to symbolize a racist, anti-Semitic regime. It was a regime bent on German domination and based on racial superiority.

Owens propelled himself forward and began flying down the track. At the key moment, he bent his legs, launched into the air, and took flight. Some 26.5 feet (8.1 m) later, he landed again, sending a spray of sand into the air. It was enough for a gold medal in the long jump event. When Jesse Owens's feet smashed back

THE COMPLEXITIES OF RACISM

The media sometimes portrays Germans in 1936 as uniformly racist, in contrast with Owens's fellow Americans. But the reality is more complicated. Racism was severe in the United States. Owens was cheered on in Berlin by German crowds as they watched him win and break records. People begged him for his autograph. He was treated as a celebrity. Both German dictator Adolf Hitler and US president Franklin Delano Roosevelt refused to congratulate him, however. Owens complained about getting better treatment in Nazi Germany than in the United States of America.

down to Earth, they also struck a blow against the Nazis' racial theories.

Owens would go on to win a total of four gold medals during the 1936 Olympic Games. He broke several records. Germany's dictator, Adolf Hitler, was sure that the German white race was superior to all others. Yet it was Jesse Owens, the grandson of a slave, who accomplished incredible things at the 1936 Olympics.

Owens's Olympic victories made him one of the most celebrated US athletes of all time.

RACE IS THE REASON?

Owens's spectacular performance at the Olympics provided a strong counterexample to the Nazi theories of white superiority. But in explaining Owens's victories, even his own countrymen resorted to racist ideas, discriminating against Owens for his race. American team coach Dean Cromwell suggested Africans had an innate edge in athletics. He said African American athletes were "closer to the primitive . . . it was not so long ago that his ability to sprint and jump was a life and death matter to him in the jungle."[1] Other Americans, such as Yale University track coach Albert McGall and X-ray specialist E. Albert Kinley, said blacks had anatomical differences that gave them an athletic edge. One example they cited was having longer heel bones. Such pseudoscientific ideas about race had been used to justify a wide range of racist beliefs. These ideas were often considered mainstream science at the

RETURNING HOME

On his return to the United States, entertainers, advertisers, and politicians snubbed Owens. To avoid poverty, Owens staged exhibitions. He ran against horses and dogs. He also worked as a playground director in Cleveland, Ohio. "People said it was degrading for an Olympic champion to run against a horse, but what was I supposed to do?" Owens said. "I had four gold medals, but you can't eat four gold medals."[2]

time, but it is clear that prejudices and biases played bigger parts in this work than actual scientific inquiry.

Some people used pseudoscience to predict Africans would eventually die out. Frederick Hoffman was a statistician for a life insurance company. He published an influential book called *Race Traits and Tendencies of the American Negro* in 1896. Hoffman compared death rates between African Americans and whites. He also compared disease rates. He found enormous disparities. However, his analysis neglected to include poverty rates between whites and blacks. It also ignored lack of access to health care. It did not factor in the effects of widespread discrimination. Instead, his report simply linked these differences to race. When Hoffman presented his statistical data, the scientific community largely accepted it. He concluded that "the tendency of the Negro race has been downward. This tendency must lead to a still greater mortality. And in the end, cause the extinction of the race."[3]

In the same year Hoffman published his book, the US Supreme Court sanctioned legal separation of the races by its ruling in *Plessy v. Ferguson*. The ruling held that separate but equal facilities did not violate the US Constitution. Schools, stores, and a wide variety of other places could be designated for either blacks or whites.

In reality, these separate spaces were far from equal. Facilities for African Americans were typically in much worse condition. The rules of segregation relegated African Americans to second-class citizenship.

Responses to Owens's victories and to racial pseudoscience provide a clear example of the poor reasoning behind racist thinking. The idea that Africans were a weaker race had helped the Supreme Court—then composed only of white people—justify segregation in 1896. Yet the idea that Africans were physically stronger was also used as an explanation for Owens's victories at the Olympic Games. Both arguments use race as a justification, but for opposite conclusions, and both theories were the product of racist thinking.

EXAMINING RACIAL DIFFERENCES

Cromwell's reasoning that Africans had an athletic edge linked to their race was incorrect. But in 1936, few people challenged such racial science as an explanation. Montague Cobb was an exception. He was an African American anthropologist and physician working in the 1930s. He measured Owens's body, including his feet, legs, and chest. Cobb concluded Owens did not have the "Negroid type of calf, foot and heel bone" that supposedly gave blacks a speed advantage.[4] Cobb compared Owens

Following *Plessy v. Ferguson*, the segregation of schools and other places became enshrined in US law.

with other athletes. Cobb's conclusion was that black athletes did not have special traits. Nor did they have physical characteristics that would make them more fit than other races.

Cobb did not stop there. He also said there was no physical marker for race at all, noting, "there is not a single physical characteristic, including skin color, which all the Negro stars have in common which definitely classify them as Negroes."[5] He compared black athletes with white athletes and compared black athletes with other black athletes. Cobb concluded there was not one racial biological factor that could explain athletic ability.

RACE IS NOT A GENETIC CODE

The science of genetics has backed up Cobb's work. A person's genetic code is a sequence of chemicals within each of his or her body's cells. These sequences are called genes. The genetic code helps

BASKETBALL AND RACE

Although some people still attribute athletic ability in basketball to race, the history of who dominated the sport undermines that theory. In the 1930s, Jewish teams were the heroes of the court. In 1992, America's Olympic "Dream Team" was almost entirely African American. A decade later, almost 20 percent of NBA starters were foreign born.[6] The number one draft pick in 2002, Yao Ming, was Chinese. Cultural aspects within an environment, such as a sport's popularity and accessibility, are better explanations of the demographics of sports than superficial features such as skin color.

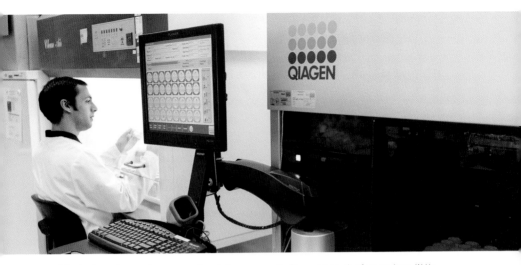

Work done in modern genetics labs suggests the concept of race has little real-world basis in a person's genes.

determine that person's physical traits. Every person has his or her own unique genetic code. People receive some elements of their genetic codes from their biological fathers and others from their biological mothers. Genetic scientists have found that the level of genetic variation among humans has nothing to do with race. In other words, an African American person's genetic code may differ just as much from that of another African American as it does from that of a white person.

The human level of genetic variation is tiny. Humans are among the most similar of all species, genetically speaking. Scientists can test this. They look at strands of DNA, the chemical that carries genetic information in human cells. They compare people's genetic codes. Genetically speaking, different races of humanity don't exist. Biologically, the concept of race is a myth. Humans are one people in the eyes of science.

Anthropologists have determined that human life originated in Africa. Humans migrated. They spread out all over the world. There are some human traits that are very old. Others are new and have evolved over time. Some of the older traits include human intelligence, athletic ability, and artistic and musical talent. People mixed with each other and passed along these early human genetic traits.

Over time, random changes in DNA, called mutations, have caused minor variations among human populations. Traits such as skin color are relatively recent. They are a result of positive selection, which is the process by which new helpful traits sweep through a population. Very few genes are involved in these newer traits. People

THE SUPREME COURT DETERMINES RACE

Whereas race may not have a genetic marker, it is a very real social construct. The US Supreme Court made a determination on who was included under the umbrella of protection for racial discrimination laws in the 1987 case *Shaare Tefila Congregation v. Cobb*.

When a Jewish synagogue was vandalized with swastikas, common Nazi symbols, it had to be determined whether or not antidiscrimination statutes could be applied. The court decided that physical appearance alone did not determine race. It said that although Jews were viewed as Caucasian, they were still protected under racial discrimination laws.

who lived in areas with less sunlight, such as northern Europe, lost their ability to produce dark melanin. Melanin is a pigment in skin. In areas of the world with higher sun exposure, such as Africa, melanin continued to work. It created darker skin as a form of protection from the sun's ultraviolet rays.

As humans migrated and mixed throughout the last 100,000 years, the dispersing groups remained genetically similar to each other. Factors that affect traits such as intellect, artistry, talent, and athletics stemmed from the original population of humanity in Africa. Some superficial traits, such as skin color, stemmed from geographic location. Therefore, the idea of race as a clearly distinct scientific identity doesn't add up.

| DISCUSSION STARTERS |

- How can people tell the difference between science and pseudoscience?

- How does the idea of race as a scientific concept differ from the idea of race as a cultural concept?

- Besides skin color, what types of minor variations exist among human beings?

CHAPTER TWO

HUMAN DIVISIONS PRIOR TO RACE

Over the course of history, societies have always found ways to organize and divide groups of people. Many factors have been used to draw these divisions. But the use of race to group and divide people is actually a relatively recent development. Economic status, land ownership, and religion were all used for this purpose before the modern conception of race arose.

SLAVERY BEFORE RACE

Enslaved peoples have long occupied the lowest rung on societies' economic ladders. Slavery in its earliest forms had nothing to do with what is now called race. It was based on power and economic status. Those in power, the wealthy, enslaved those at the bottom.

Slavery was in place in ancient Greece as well as in Rome. The Greek slavery system held humans in bondage to a master. Those enslaved were forced to do physical labor. Slavery was widespread. Some households in these societies had three or four slaves.[1]

Unlike later systems of slavery, the ancient Greek system was not based on race. The society saw all foreigners as eligible slaves. They viewed anyone who was not Greek as inferior. Slaves were typically captives taken in war. They belonged to a variety of different ethnicities.

Most were what would now be considered white. This system did not view slavery as a lifelong identity, and it did not hold that the child of a slave was also a slave.

Still, slaves were treated with cruelty. They were prisoners, and they were powerless. They were expected to perform labor, but not for their entire lives. Eventually, many were given freedom. Some even inherited family wealth.

Slavery was also present in the early Middle Ages. The British enslaved Slavic peoples from central and eastern Europe. The word *slavery* has its origins in the word Slav. Religion, not race, became a reason for slavery. The Christian church eventually opposed the enslavement of Christians. Converting to Christianity safeguarded people from becoming enslaved.

SLAVE RECOGNITION IN ANCIENT ROME

Roman slavery was not based on race. Roman slaves worked in all areas of the community. They could be found in private homes, mines, factories, and farms. Since the slaves were not all of one particular race, and because they worked everywhere, they blended in with the population. It could be hard to know who was a citizen and who was a slave.

The Roman Senate considered a plan for slave uniforms so that slaves could be easily identified. It was rejected. The Senate feared that once the slaves themselves realized how many slaves there were, they might join together to overthrow their rulers. One in three people living in Italy was a slave.

Ancient navies sometimes used the rowing power of slaves to propel their boats.

Slavery was not based on race until the Age of Exploration, in the 1500s. During this era, Europeans launched voyages to the Americas, set up colonies, and began a transatlantic trade system. The Atlantic slave trade involved vast numbers of Africans. They were not selected because they were war captives or prisoners. They were selected because they were African. Once enslaved, they held no power and were at the bottom of the economic hierarchy.

LAND OWNERSHIP

Ownership of land proved to be another way to divide people. Those who owned land held greater power, wealth, and status than those who did not. Ownership of land created a separate social and economic class of people. The European system of feudalism in the early Middle Ages created a power hierarchy in which land-owning lords were at the top and the people of the peasantry were at the bottom.

The lords, or the nobility, had the power to make decisions. They also took responsibility for the serfs who worked their land. The nobility often provided serfs with housing, food, and protection. The elite class believed it had a divine right to rule. Status was passed down from generation to generation. As time went on, this notion

In the feudal system, landless peasants worked the property of wealthy landlords.

of superiority by nature was widely accepted and helped justify the hierarchy.

RELIGIOUS DIVISIONS

Religion has also long been a vehicle for division. It has been an impetus for war, violence, and expulsion from territories. Christians, Muslims, and Jews all sought to control land. There was a period of time, however, when all three groups lived on the Iberian Peninsula, present-day Spain and Portugal, in harmony.

This occurred when the Moors controlled the region. The term Moors referred to Muslim people from North Africa as well as Arabs of the Middle East. It was not a strictly racial descriptor. It included black, white, and brown people alike. Moors spread throughout southern Europe. They conquered the Iberian Peninsula starting in the 700s CE.

Moors contributed many advanced cultural and scientific ideas. Arab astronomers knew that Earth was a sphere as early as the 800s CE. They calculated its circumference and diameter quite accurately. On the Iberian Peninsula, Moors built libraries at a time when public libraries were nonexistent throughout the rest of Europe. They also improved agriculture by introducing irrigation systems. They created sanitation systems. Moors

built several advanced
cities, including Granada
and Seville. Moors also
made education accessible
and available to all in
their Spanish territories.
The rest of Europe was
still mostly illiterate, as
reading was considered
the business of monks
and priests.

Moors interacted peacefully with Jews and Christians for hundreds of years. The groups fully participated in an intellectual and cultural exchange. Some Jews even acted as trusted advisers to Muslim rulers. The different religious groups did not view each other as threats. They worked cooperatively to build their society. But intellectual progress did not save the diverse groups from conflict forever. In the end, issues over religion pitted the people of the Iberian Peninsula against each other and led to war.

THE LEAD-UP TO A NEW WORLD ORDER

Several ingredients soon mixed to create a recipe for a new world order. First, the bubonic plague of 1348 killed

The architectural legacy of the Moors can still be seen in Spain today.

approximately 25 million people in Europe.[2] It led to the breakdown of social order as the disease destroyed families and communities. Famine and wars continued to ravage the survivors, creating a vacuum for social upheaval.

Next, the Christian effort known as the Reconquista slowly recaptured the Iberian Peninsula from the Moors. Christian Europeans, especially in Portugal, began establishing direct trading and diplomatic contacts with Africa. By the middle of the 1400s, Africans were being sent to the Portuguese prince, Henry, as gifts. Later, Africans were sent as slaves.

The Reconquista came to a conclusion in 1492, when King Ferdinand and Queen Isabella of Spain took Granada from the Moors. It had been the Moors' final power center in Europe. Originally, the Christian monarchy claimed Moorish culture and institutions would remain and be protected. However, in 1502, the Spanish crown demanded the expulsion of the Moors from the Iberian Peninsula. The only possible way they could stay was if they agreed to convert to Christianity. Even those who did convert were not actually protected. Many of them were later charged with secretly remaining faithful to Islam. The ensuing 50 years would see more than one million Moors forced out of Spain. Religious factions drew new lines of division. Christian Spanish and Portuguese people were at the apex of the power pyramid.

Jews faced similar expulsions. They were also expected to convert to Christianity. Not only were Jews considered a threat because of religious differences, but they were also viewed as economic competitors by Christians. Although Jews had lived on the Iberian Peninsula for hundreds of years, they were not allowed to work in so-called Christian trades within Christian areas of the peninsula. These trades included masonry and carpentry.

By the end of the 1400s, the system of feudalism had begun to disappear. It became possible for Christian Europeans to rise from the peasant class to the higher merchant class. This again led to the naming of Jews as economic competitors. Approximately 200,000 Jews refused to convert.[3] They were ordered to leave Spain. All their property was confiscated.

These events placed Spain in a position of great power right at the moment that Christopher Columbus launched his first expedition in 1492. His arrival in the Americas led to a new world order and the rise of a new form of slavery. Human divisions would not only include previous demarcations such as economic standing, land ownership, and religion. These divisions would soon be dominated by a new factor: race.

| DISCUSSION STARTERS |

- Are the three factors discussed in this chapter—economic standing, land ownership, and religion—still used to divide people today? If so, how?

- Can you think of any other factors by which people have historically been divided?

- Did anything surprise you about the nature of slavery in ancient Greece and Rome?

Hundreds of years of fierce battles eventually brought the Iberian
Peninsula back under Spanish and Portuguese control.

CHAPTER THREE

COLONIALISM, SLAVERY, AND RACE

Christopher Columbus's 1492 voyage across the Atlantic Ocean would help forever change the way societies thought about race. But the journey's original goal had little to do with important social issues. Instead, Columbus's key motivation was money.

When Spain's King Ferdinand and Queen Isabella agreed to fund his voyage, a contract was written with specific terms. One was that Columbus could keep one-tenth of all the profits he reaped.[1] The rest would go back to the Spanish Crown. The stakes were high. Columbus sought to win those profits by any means possible. He set out to find riches in the Indies, an area encompassing what are now known as East Asia and South Asia.

PLANTING WEALTH

The terms of Columbus's contract did not specify what type of assets he was to find. Columbus was hoping to find reserves of gold. But he did not end up in the Indies as planned. Instead, he arrived at the Caribbean Islands and the Americas. These areas became commonly known as the New World. In these lands, previously unknown to him, gold and silver were in limited supply.

Columbus made a total of four voyages to the Americas over the course of the next decade. To increase income for the Spanish Crown and himself, he embarked on a twofold plan. First, he began enslaving the native people he found in the New World. He sent groups of them back to Spain.

The other source of wealth was the land itself. It became clear that although the land was not rich with gold, it held value in other ways. The plantation system, involving large farms supervised by overseers, allowed the

A European artist's depiction of Columbus presenting captured Native Americans to the king and queen of Spain

Spanish to produce massive profits. The Spanish farmed sugarcane. Merchants shipped the sugarcane and other goods between the Americas and Europe. This system was dependent on slave labor. The new form of slavery starkly divided European masters from Native American slaves. Such a division would lay the groundwork for even more widespread forms of slavery, as well as race-based justifications for the practice, in the centuries to come.

CONTRACT FOR CRUELTY

Slavery was a key component in the plantation system. European overseers subordinated and dehumanized slaves. Columbus labeled the people of the Carib tribe as cannibals, though there is no evidence to support this assertion. These people lived on the islands now known as the Lesser Antilles. Columbus described the Caribs as subhumans. As such, the Spanish deemed them worthy of enslavement and violence. They were rendered powerless, exploited, and destroyed. When native people fought back against this oppression, the Spanish used their resistance as a reason to further demonize them.

Another Native American tribe, the Tainos, also suffered at the hands of the Spanish. The Tainos lived on Hispaniola, the island that is now home to the Dominican Republic and Haiti. At first, Columbus described the

Tainos as a loving people. He felt they would be ideal candidates for Christian conversion. But he also ordered all Tainos aged 14 and up to bring him a quota of gold every three months. The Tainos were doomed to fail, as there was not much gold to be discovered in the area. Those who could not meet the quota faced brutal punishments. Spanish overseers cut off their limbs, tore them apart with attack dogs, and let them bleed to death. These acts of terror were meant to strike fear into the hearts of those being subordinated.

INTENTIONS AND OUTCOMES

Spanish religious leader Bartolomé de Las Casas was dismayed at the cruelty shown toward slaves in the Caribbean. The treatment of the native people had had dramatic effects. The Spanish came and conquered. Disease,

LAS CASAS'S REGRET

In a humanitarian effort to end Native American slavery, Las Casas suggested Africans replace them. He believed the Africans were more fit for hard labor. Las Casas came to regret his statements. He felt that all slavery was immoral. Writing in the third-person, he said:

This note to give license to bring black slaves to these lands was first given by the cleric Casas, not taking into account the injustice with which the Portuguese captured and enslaved them; then, having discovered this, he would not for all the world advocate this, for he held enslaving them both unjust and tyrannical; and the same goes for the Indians.[2]

slavery, and Spanish brutality ravaged the population. Las Casas witnessed the atrocities. From 1509 until his death in 1566, he tried to advocate for the native people. He could not justify what they were enduring at the hands of the Spanish.

When Las Casas spoke about protecting the Native Americans from the abuses of slavery, the crown asked him who would take on the labor of the plantation system. He suggested that Africans might be able to withstand the work better. African slavery had already been introduced in Europe 50 years prior to Columbus's conquest. The Portuguese were selling Africans as captives at auctions.

King Ferdinand of Spain passed a decree allowing Africans to be sent to the New World. The Spanish used methods of terror, including public beating and branding by fire, as ways to instill fear and obedience in the African people they captured. Africans were rounded up, tied down, chained together, and thrown into ships to be brought to the Americas. They were fed scraps of rotten food, barely enough to keep them alive. Those who didn't survive were thrown overboard. Sharks followed the ships, waiting for more food. It is estimated that approximately 2.5 million enslaved Africans survived the journey to the Spanish colonies between the 1500s and the early 1800s.[3] This journey became known as the Middle Passage.

Those who survived were sold. Families were torn apart. Mothers were sold separately from their children. Slaves had no rights. Whips and cutlasses kept them under strict control. Owners had absolute power over the people they enslaved.

Vicious assaults and attacks were used to subordinate the African slaves. Europeans began to view them as a separate race or even as a lesser variation of humanity. The success of the plantation system depended on slave labor. As a result, the economics of this system drove racism. In part to justify the practice of slavery, the ideology of race took root.

| DISCUSSION STARTERS |

- Columbus Day, designated in honor of the explorer's arrival in the Americas, is officially recognized by the United States on the second Monday of October. Many people have criticized the holiday because of Columbus's treatment of the native people he found in the Americas. What is your opinion on Columbus Day?

- This chapter discusses how the desire for wealth helped drive the division of people based on race. Does this factor continue to divide people today? How so?

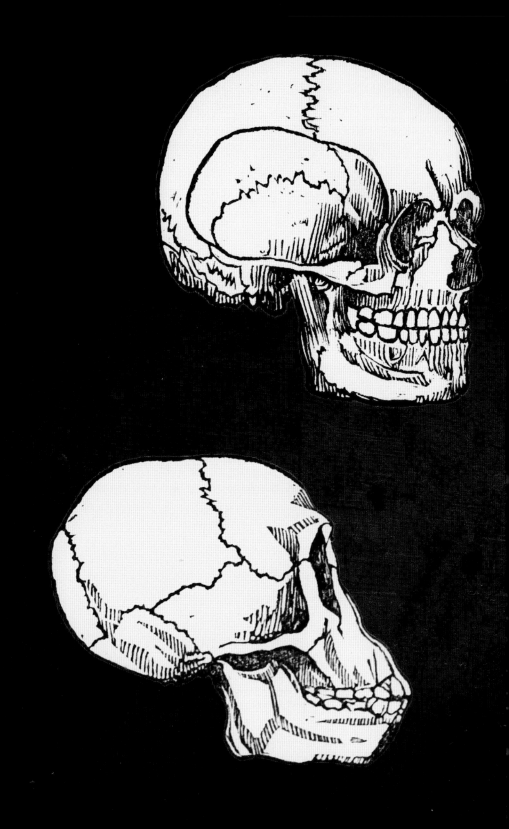

CHAPTER FOUR

EARLY SCHOOLS OF THOUGHT ON RACE

Many thinkers of the colonial era developed theories to justify the treatment of enslaved African people. Often they proposed ideas of race that steered justifications away from plantation owners' greed and profits. These various schools of thought were more acceptable to the oppressors. People used science, religion, and philosophy to explain why people of different races should be treated differently.

SCIENCE CEMENTS RACE

Economic motivation led to the modern notions of race and racism, but science was used to help justify these notions. Such studies were pseudoscientific. One of these explanations was known as preadamism. This idea was closely linked to Christianity. It was adopted by some thinkers in the 1700s. It suggested there were multiple strains of mankind. Adam, from the creation story of the Bible, was seen as the ancestor of Christians and Europeans. Preadamite thinkers argued there were earlier strains of humanity, before Adam. The earlier versions were less civilized. They were primitive humans. They were closely linked to animals. Europeans suggested that Africans might be the descendants of the primitive humans.

In the late 1700s, pseudoscientific theories gained popularity through the writing of the German professor Johann Friedrich Blumenbach. He was a student of Carl Linnaeus, who had suggested that there were four races of mankind. Linnaeus concluded that the four groups were different from each other but did not assign them value.

Blumenbach was an early proponent of the idea that the notion of race had a biological basis.

Blumenbach took this assertion a few steps further. For him, physical appearance determined racial categorization. His racial structure included Caucasian as the white race, Mongolian as the yellow race, Malayan as the brown race, Ethiopian as the black race, and American as the red race. He decided that people from the Caucasus Mountains in Russia had the most beautiful skulls and skin; as a result, for him the so-called Caucasians were the superior race. Due to its nonscientific origins, current social scientists often avoid the term Caucasian.

Blumenbach's pseudoscience was racist, but it was also widely accepted. He felt that the original, pure man must have been white and that lesser versions of pure humans had darker skin. He argued that it was easier to make white skin darker with sunlight, but more difficult to turn dark skin lighter. Therefore, he said, white skin must have been pure and dark skin a degeneration.

In the 1800s, race science was of keen interest to the American people as pressure to abolish slavery mounted. Some sought to justify slavery with science, even if the evidence for their results was flimsy or nonexistent. One example of this came in the 1854 book *Types of Mankind* by Josiah Clark Nott and George Robins Gliddon. They followed in the footsteps of Samuel Morton, a doctor who had collected skulls from around the world and studied

FIG. 345.[559]

Orang-Outan.

FIG. 346.[561]

Hottentot Wagoner — Caffre War.

FIG. 347.[560]

Chimpanzee.

FIG. 348.[562]

Hottentot from Somerset.

FIG. 349.

Mobile Negro, 1853.

FIG. 350.

Mobile Negro, 1853.

FIG. 351.

Negro, 3200 years old [supra, pp. 250–251].

FIG. 352.

Nubian, 3200 years old.

(459)

The drawings and ideas in *Types of Mankind,* presented as factual science at the time, are today seen as wildly racist, deeply offensive, and entirely incorrect.

them through the lens of race. All three based their work primarily on skull analysis. They measured skull and brain sizes and assigned intellectual capacities to different races. Morton deemed Americans the smartest, followed by the British and the French. He placed Africans at the bottom of his hierarchy.

Types of Mankind was the best-selling science book of its time. The book found a receptive audience in the South. Some Southerners argued that because the African people were apparently inferior, they should not be allowed to participate in the nation's democracy. Further, they argued, slavery was a fitting use for these people.

RELIGION DIVIDES AND JUSTIFIES

The belief that Christianity was the only correct religion helped support the notion that anyone who was not Christian was inferior. Many Christians made converting nonbelievers part of their mission. They believed they could "civilize" those people. Converting meant effectively destroying previous cultural beliefs. It also eradicated non-Christian religions. Violence against Africans and Native Americans was sometimes justified by Christian Europeans by viewing these people as heathens.

Biblical stories also provided examples of groups of people being treated as inferior. A story in the book of

Genesis has been interpreted as a biblical authorization for slavery. The story says that Noah set up a vineyard. He got drunk and fell asleep naked. One of his three sons, Ham, found him and laughed at him. Ham tried to get his brothers to laugh at Noah too. Noah woke up furious. He cursed Ham and his descendants. He declared Ham would be a slave to the other two brothers.

Some Christians have used this story throughout history to explain that whoever is at the bottom of the social hierarchy must be a descendant of Ham. Peasants were seen as the descendants of Ham in the Middle Ages.

An engraving from a Russian Bible printed in the early 1900s shows Noah cursing his son Ham.

RACISM ON DISPLAY

The 1904 World's Fair held in Saint Louis, Missouri, marked the 100-year anniversary of the Louisiana Purchase, the US acquisition from France of a large swath of the United States. The fair was meant to celebrate the progress of the nation and the world. It was also meant to inform the fairgoers of the technological and cultural advances that had been achieved. One exhibit, organized by the fair's anthropology department, displayed living humans. Tribal people, including American Indians and Filipinos, were put on display in recreated native villages. These exhibits were designed so that fairgoers could see the "progress" of man. The tribal people were considered primitive. The fair also included an exhibit that presented an idealized version of slave life on a Southern plantation.

Fairgoers posed for pictures with the people in these exhibits. They would compare skin colors. Those on display were regarded as subjects of curiosity. They were meant to exemplify unsophisticated races. Spectators were meant to compare themselves against them.

An exhibit at the 1904 World's Fair featured people brought from the Philippines, the Pacific Island nation that was at the time a recent US territorial acquisition.

The Slavic slaves were considered descendants. Then, in the 1400s, Africans were assigned this curse by Christians. The story allowed for one branch of the human family to be treated as a lesser group. It was used as biblical justification for Europeans to mistreat and enslave other peoples, including Africans.

PHILOSOPHERS AND RACE

The Enlightenment was a European intellectual movement of the 1600s and 1700s. It supported the idea that humanity could be improved through rational thinking. It rejected traditional authority. It changed the way science and politics were viewed. Philosophers believed education and environment could improve people. They argued that people's abilities were not based on the circumstances of their birth alone. Instead, they could be cultivated. Philosophers such as David Hume, Jean-Jacques Rousseau, John Locke, and Voltaire were extremely influential in this movement.

Philosophers of the Enlightenment valued liberty, equality, and fraternity. These democratic principles were at the center of the American Revolution (1775–1783) and the French Revolution (1787–1799). People no longer viewed themselves as subjects of royalty. They saw themselves as humans with their own individual power to learn and use reason. Having a mind meant having power and independence.

But although philosophers supported democracy and freedom, many also accepted the practice of slavery. They were bystanders to the exploitation of Africans. Philosophers appealed to the notion of race to explain this disconnect. Locke, for example, wondered if Africans were the same species as Europeans. Those who subscribed to these theories often considered Africans animalistic, violent, and ignorant.

Moral philosopher Immanuel Kant believed in humanism, saying that people must respect each other. He also believed in the concept of duty. Kant said the only thing that gives an action moral

THE UNENLIGHTENED PHILOSOPHERS

Enlightenment philosophers David Hume and Immanuel Kant are considered some of the greatest minds of modern times. However, their own words in the mid-1700s demonstrate deeply racist ideologies.

On listening to Johannes Gottfried Kraus, the rector of the University of Wittenberg, describe a report that was from an African, Kant swiftly dismissed it. His basis was that "this fellow was quite black from head to toe, a clear proof that what he said was stupid."[1]

Hume had similar racist perceptions. He wrote, "I am apt to suspect the Negroes, and in general all other species of men to be naturally inferior to the whites. There never was any civilized nation of any other complection than white, nor even any individual eminent in action or speculation."[2]

Immanuel Kant is widely considered one of the central figures in modern philosophy.

worth is the motive that is behind the action. That was seen as more meaningful than the success of the action. However, he and several philosophers contradicted their own theories. Their ideas were never universally applied. Although they said they believed in equal rights, they also clearly believed white people were superior to black people.

Kant published anthropological and physical geography papers. In them, he described a four-tiered structure of human classification. It was a racially restrictive view. The top tier included white Europeans. They alone were capable of being fully enlightened. The other rungs were not capable of the same level of reasoning. They included Asians, Africans, and Native Americans.

DISCUSSION STARTERS

- Does knowing the racial attitudes of major figures from the past, such as renowned philosophers, change the way you think about these figures?

- Based on what you've read, how did thinking about race change between the time of Christopher Columbus and the time of the Enlightenment?

- This chapter discusses how people used religion to justify slavery. Later in history, people such as Martin Luther King Jr. would use religion to justify equality and civil rights. What do you think this says about religion as a tool to justify social aims?

CHAPTER FIVE

SLAVERY IN THE COLONIES

In the 1600s, at the time England began setting up colonies along the East Coast of North America, philosophers, religious leaders, and scientific authorities were making claims that different races of humanity existed. They convinced many of their fellow Europeans that nonwhites were not as sophisticated as whites. They argued Africans were animalistic, less evolved, and biologically different. Such racist claims had stemmed in part from the rise of the slave trade and the plantation systems set up by Europeans in their colonies in the Americas.

The colonial system relied on slave labor in order to thrive. It created massive wealth and power for European nations. The dependence on slave labor resulted in the search for a moral justification for the practice. Race provided that justification. In other words, the modern American ideology of race developed as a consequence of slavery.

SEARCHING FOR CHEAP LABOR

One of the earliest systems of labor used in England's colonies was indentured servitude. Indentured servants—typically whites—traveled to the Virginia Colony in the 1600s. They were poor, and the New World offered them a chance at a better life. They agreed to labor as indentured servants, often for four to seven years. In exchange, they received passage to America, a place to live, and a chance at freedom if they survived their contract. They worked on tobacco plantations. Many endured inhumane treatment, cruelty, brutality, and exploitation. If they tried to advocate for themselves, retaliate, or run away, their terms of service could be extended further.

Once indentured servants completed their terms of service, they were released and given the rights of freedom. Their contracts sometimes included the promise of a piece of land, as well as food, tools, and livestock. This gave servants a chance to create modest lives for themselves as free men.

Plantation owners in the colonies claimed huge

1676 REBELLION

Many freed indentured servants in America felt unsatisfied. They were white men who did not own land. In 1676, they launched a rebellion against the colonial government of Virginia. They plundered the property of the elite. The royal governor went into hiding on the eastern shore of Virginia. The rebellion ended abruptly and accomplished little. The white lower class did not gain political power. However, it did plant fear in the minds of the rich and powerful. White and black indentured servants had joined the rebellion, fighting side by side. The ruling class feared future united uprisings. It worked to make the racial divides between enslaved people and free people clearer to avoid having this happen again.

chunks of land. They realized it would take extensive labor to work these huge estates. Indentured servants became expensive, and the arduous work led to a reduced number of people volunteering to become indentured servants. Plantation owners looked to Africa for a new labor source. However, unlike the indentured servants, workers from Africa would not be coming voluntarily. After purchasing an enslaved person, a plantation manager owned him or her for life. Plantation owners soon realized the onetime purchase of a slave would net more profit in the long run than using indentured servants.

LAWS TURN OPPRESSION INTO INFERIORITY

The colonies began to pass laws that made slaves chattel, or personal property. Chattel slavery held that people were property that could be bought, sold, traded, or inherited. Maryland slave laws enacted in 1664 made slavery a state that one could be born into. Thus, enslaved African women were considered valuable. They served multiple purposes for plantation owners. They would be forced not only to work, but also to have children.

The Virginia Slave Codes of 1705 cemented the notion of race. These laws made it clear that the society's rules were based on individuals' racial backgrounds. The terminology in these statutes was different from that in earlier laws. People of European descent were now referred to as *white* rather than as Christian or Englishmen. Slaves were referred to as Negroes. The new laws made distinctions based on skin color explicit.

The Virginia Slave Codes helped spread the so-called "one-drop rule." This rule said one drop of African blood—that is, a single African ancestor—made a person black. This made female African slaves even more valuable. Regardless of the father's race, the child would be a slave. The law set up clear lines between who would be considered white and who would be considered black. It also established the consequences of those identities.

Chattel slavery in America differed from slavery in the Spanish colonies. In the Spanish colonies, biracial people were recognized as biracial and not categorized as black. The one-drop rule did not apply. The social hierarchy allowed for intermarriage.

VIRGINIA SLAVE CODES OF 1705

The Virginia Slave Codes were extremely clear about the status of slaves—including their races:

All Negro, mulatto and Indian slaves . . . within this dominion, shall be held . . . to be real estate. If any slave resist his master . . . (resulting in the master) correcting such slave, and (the slave) shall happen to be killed in such correction . . . the master . . . shall be free of all punishment . . . as if such incident had never happened.[1]

Historical illustrations sometimes show smiling or joyful slaves, but in reality the life of an enslaved person was harsh and brutal.

The social order held Peninsulares, or Spanish-born landowners, at the top. They were the elite. They made the laws and worked closely with the Spanish Crown. Next came the Criollos. This title typically referred to Spanish Americans. They were the descendants of the Peninsulares and owned ranches and mines. They were part of the elite class. Since there were so few Peninsulares, some Native Americans and mixed-race people were entitled to be a part of privileged society. The term *Indio* described someone of Native American descent. Many of the elite Native Americans were accepted into Spanish society through intermarriage. Mestizos were of mixed race, one parent being Spanish and the other being Native American. People known as Negroes, or African slaves, were at the bottom of the social pyramid. They had few rights or privileges.

JEFFERSON AND RACE

Thomas Jefferson was one of the leading figures behind the establishment of the United States of America in 1776. He served as the nation's third president, but he is perhaps most famous for writing the Declaration of Independence. That document, written to explain why England's colonies were breaking away and forming an independent nation, includes passages on the equality of human beings:

> *We hold these truths to be self-evident, that all men are created equal, that they are endowed by their Creator with certain unalienable Rights, that among these are Life, Liberty and the pursuit of Happiness.*[2]

The signers of the Declaration of Independence endorsed a document that proclaimed equality among all men, yet many of them owned slaves.

Though he wrote about equality, Jefferson was a leader and thinker in the midst of a philosophical contradiction. He called on the writings of the philosophers of the Enlightenment to support the notion of democracy, yet he owned slaves. He reconciled this moral issue by turning to race as a justification for taking rights away from Africans while at the same time demanding rights for white Americans. He wrote, "blacks . . . are inferior to the whites in the endowments both in body and mind."[3] This supposed inferiority made it acceptable to own these people as slaves.

Whereas laws demoted blacks to an inferior status, they simultaneously protected and raised the status of whites. Slaves found themselves on the lowest rung of the social and political hierarchy. Even the poorest whites could consider themselves superior to the entire class of enslaved people. The notion of race benefited whites economically as well as socially.

| DISCUSSION STARTERS |

- Based on what you've read, how did laws play a part in defining America's cultural concept of race?

- How might the effects of a person being enslaved continue to impact that person's descendants in future generations?

- From what you've read, in what ways did the practice of slavery change between ancient Greece and colonial America? How did the notion of race play a role in these changes?

CHAPTER SIX

RACE AND NATIVE AMERICANS

The British colonial system in America was creating wealth. The land produced profit, and settlers were hungry for more land. They pushed many Native American tribes out of their traditional coastal homelands. As the settlers continued to claim more land, they pushed more tribes farther west.

JEFFERSON AND NATIVE AMERICANS

Thomas Jefferson wrote the book *Notes on the State of Virginia* in 1781 as a response to questions about Virginia posed to him by a French official. He relates information about the rivers and land. He reports on the state's natural resources, politics, and trade. He also describes the people.

Jefferson's work discusses several tribes, including the Monacans and the Powhatans. Jefferson's opinions about the Native American people differed from his views on Africans. He did not perceive the Native Americans as racially inferior. They were considered brave warriors who were protecting their lands. Jefferson said that "their activity of mind is equal to ours in the same situation."[1]

Jefferson and the colonists viewed Native Americans as naturally white people whose skin turned brown due to their exposure to the sun. The prejudice against the

Native people was seen as being less about race than about culture. Even through the lens of the Enlightenment, many whites in Europe and America believed a perceived cultural inferiority was a valid reason for discrimination.

The Enlightenment philosophers claimed people could improve themselves through education and hard work. They believed it was possible for people to become more sophisticated and cultured through logic and reason. Many whites believed that one step toward elevating the Native American people was to "civilize" them by introducing them to Christianity.

Jefferson viewed the racial status of whites, blacks, and Native Americans differently.

THE PROCLAMATION OF 1763

However, many Native American nations didn't want to become "civilized." Each nation had its own culture, spiritual beliefs, and family structures. Their ancestors had lived on the continent for thousands of years. They defended themselves and their cultures.

When it became clear Native Americans would not willingly hand over land to the British colonists, perceptions of them changed swiftly. The Native Americans were seen as being in the way of colonial expansion. They were impeding the potential profits of colonial landholders. They were quickly labeled as savages who had to be driven off the land or even exterminated.

Tension between the two groups escalated. This was problematic because the Native Americans were critical trading partners for some colonists. To contain the problem, the British Parliament passed the Proclamation of 1763. It stated no whites were allowed to settle west of the Appalachian Mountains. Still, the white settlers wanted that land. They sought it in order to gain more profit. They felt betrayed by England, leading to more colonial resentment against the mother country. Colonists began to argue Native Americans belonged to a different, uncivilized race. White men viewed themselves as more entitled to the land simply because they were white.

AN ATTEMPT TO CONFORM

The colonists successfully won their independence from the British in the American Revolution in 1783. After the revolution, many Native American groups chose to cooperate with the newly established United States of America. They hoped for peace.

The people of the Cherokee tribe in particular transformed their culture and were viewed as "civilized Indians." The Cherokees had signed treaties ceding most of their land to the United States. They became farmers. They were plantation owners. Some even followed the American custom of owning slaves.

The Cherokees not only accepted the American economic system but also adopted its political and social systems. They established a government and a constitution based on the US model. They created similar educational

MANIFEST DESTINY

The phrase *Manifest Destiny* originated in an 1845 article in an American journal called the *Democratic Review*. The article stated that US expansion would be "the fulfillment of our Manifest Destiny to overspread the continent allotted by Providence for the free development of our yearly multiplying millions."[2] This meant that expanding across North America was the Americans' obvious mission from God.

Manifest Destiny became a justification for the removal of all Native Americans that stood in the way. Claiming that God wanted white Americans to take over the land made any actions taken toward that goal acceptable.

systems, and their children attended school. There were many marriages between Cherokee people and white people.

For some Cherokees, all of the efforts to conform seemed to be working. Some became prosperous. But when poor whites saw these accomplishments, many felt

The government sometimes took Native American children from their communities and placed them in boarding schools, forcing them to adapt to the dominant white culture.

anger and resentment. They wanted what the Cherokee had. They wanted land and status. They had to find a reason to justify why they should have it more than the Cherokee who had earned it. They turned to race.

THE TRAIL OF TEARS

President Andrew Jackson, elected in 1828, was a populist president. He proclaimed that he stood up for the common man. Supporters considered him an antidote to elitist politicians who did not care about their concerns. Jackson was a political outsider. He found strong support among poor, landless white men. Jackson demanded the Cherokees give up their land so it could be redistributed to poor whites. The Cherokees had followed

The US government forced Native Americans out of their homelands and into distant reservations.

the rules. Still, resentment against their race was used to justify the actions against them.

Jackson signed the Indian Removal Act in May 1830. It allowed the government to force Native Americans to leave their traditional lands inside state borders. The removed people would be granted unsettled lands west of the Mississippi River. When the Cherokee refused, Jackson explicitly gave race as a reason for their inferiority: "They have neither the intelligence, the industry, the moral habits, nor the desire of improvement which are essential to any favorable change in their condition. Established in the midst of another and a superior race. . . . they must . . . disappear."[4]

The Cherokee felt betrayed. After doing everything they could to assimilate and coexist peacefully with the white Americans, they were still characterized as savages. They fought vigorously against removal. They even appealed to the US court system to defend them. In the end, they were forced at gunpoint to travel west along what the Cherokee people called the Trail of Tears. Approximately 15,000 Cherokee were forced to relocate.[5] More than 4,000 of them died on the arduous journey.[6] Jackson's message was made clear. The policy of the US government would be that US lands belonged to white Americans.

| DISCUSSION STARTERS |

- For decades, President Andrew Jackson appeared on the US $20 bill. In April 2016, the US Treasury announced abolitionist Harriet Tubman would soon replace him. What is your opinion on having figures such as Jackson, who were historically significant yet held racist views, on US currency?

- How did early US settlers justify discrimination against Native American people? How does this compare with the era's justifications for slavery?

CHAPTER SEVEN

RACE AND IMMIGRANTS

In the 1800s, vast numbers of immigrants found a new home in the United States. The majority were poor, leaving their home countries in part to escape economic or societal challenges. They hoped to improve their lives in America. But many—including those who today would be considered white—were subjected to racial discrimination.

These types of racial discrimination were strongly linked with xenophobia. People in one nation sometimes judge and stereotype immigrants from other nations. The native group often has preconceived notions about the foreign group. It may feel anxiety about economic or social competition from the new arrivals. In an effort to keep the foreign groups down, the notion of race may be used as a tool for discrimination.

HATED BY THE TOP AND BOTTOM

In the 1840s, Ireland experienced a catastrophic potato famine. The failure of the potato crop to flourish over a number of years led to starvation. Thousands of Irish farmers had nothing to sell. They could not pay their laborers. The farmers and laborers were unable to pay their rents. The potato was a key food source, especially for the people of rural Ireland. Following years of crop failures, they lacked both money and food. Millions of Irish people fled the country and headed to the United States. They settled in port cities along the northeast coast, including Boston, Massachusetts.

The Irish immigrants were desperate. They were poor and often uneducated. They lacked critical career skills, but they could clean, cook, and work in factories. They often found work in servitude, serving the city's elite class. The new immigrants were willing to work for low wages. They packed in together in small houses called tenements.

An Irish man coming to the United States, *center,* awaits processing at an immigration station.

Wealthy people looked down on the immigrants, seeing them as being fit only for servitude. At the same time, many in the white working class in Boston viewed the new arrivals with disgust and anger. The Irish immigrants were often willing to do their jobs for less money. People felt this threatened their way of life and social status. Many businesses refused to hire Irish immigrants. They posted signs in their windows that said, "No Irish Need Apply."[1]

ASSIGNING ATTRIBUTES

When people sort groups into separate races, one common aspect of this sorting is the assignment of particular attributes to one race or another. In the mid-1800s, the upper class in the United States assigned the Irish immigrants many negative attributes to justify their classification as a servant race.

The Irish were categorized as angry and temperamental with a lack of self-control. The men were stereotyped as alcoholics. Irish women gained a reputation for depression and mental illness. Families were said to have had too many children. Negative portrayals of Irish people in newspapers, cartoons, and theatre productions showed them as stupid, greedy, and immoral.

Pseudoscientists believed the Irish were more closely related to apes than to other Europeans. In some cases in the United States, the Irish were classified as black. Writers in popular periodicals analyzed the shapes of their skulls and faces to suggest the Irish were more like Africans than Europeans.

BECOMING WHITE

When Irish immigrants first arrived in the United States, many people did not consider them white. But over time, Irish immigrants organized and formed strong communities. They entered politics and gained power in the government. They became strong presences in police forces and labor unions. Eventually, most in the United States considered them mainstream Americans. They are now typically identified as white.

In the 1800s, blacks and Irish immigrants in the United States shared some things in common. Both groups began their lives in the nation at the bottom of the social hierarchy. They both had low economic status. Each was regarded as a servant race. Racism and a resulting lack of opportunity kept them from improving their status in society.

IMMIGRANT GROUPS: HISTORY'S SCAPEGOATS

Immigrants in the United States have often been treated as scapegoats. They take the blame for economic troubles. They are accused of stealing jobs from US-born

The Mexican-American War resulted in the United States taking possession of a huge swath of Mexican territory in the West.

working-class whites. They have also been villainized as people who should be feared during times of war.

In the nation's early years, white Americans blamed Mexicans for impeding the country's growth. In the late 1830s, much of what is now the southwestern United States was part of Mexico. Americans wanted that land and considered it part of their Manifest Destiny to conquer it. By assigning Mexicans racist attributes, they

were made to be viewed as foreign, even when they were living in their own lands.

Once Americans perceived Mexicans as foreign, it became easy to make them scapegoats. The United States launched the Mexican-American War (1846–1848) to take over Mexican land. As were the Native Americans, Mexicans were viewed as obstacles to the American Manifest Destiny. Stephen Austin encouraged his

American countrymen to seize Texas for the United States. He stated his desire to "redeem it from the wilderness—to settle it with an intelligent honorable and enterprising people."[2] He viewed a "mongrel Spanish-Indian and negro race" as the enemy and America as "civilization and the Anglo-American race."[3] Americans entered and settled Mexico illegally and then went to war to claim it as their own. In the 1840s, one American invader, Benjamin Ide, told his men, "We are robbers, or we must be conquerors!" in order to justify taking over territories in what is now California from the Mexicans.[4]

Latinos and Latinas, people with ancestry in Mexico, Central America,

IMMIGRANT BIAS CONTINUES

An incidence of racism against Latinos gained widespread attention in the news in 2016. That summer, Republican presidential candidate Donald Trump declared that federal judge Gonzalo Curiel, who was overseeing lawsuits against Trump's for-profit education company, could not be impartial because his Mexican heritage would result in a bias against Trump. Throughout the campaign, Trump had used harsh rhetoric against immigrants from Mexico, and he had pledged to build a massive wall on the border between Mexico and the United States. Politicians from both major parties denounced Trump's statements. Republican Speaker of the House Paul Ryan described the words as "the textbook definition of a racist comment."[5] The incident suggested that bias in the United States against immigrants was still an active force in modern society.

or South America, have been common scapegoats in recent decades as well. Similar to the Irish immigrants of the 1800s, recent Mexican immigrants have been blamed for stealing jobs by being willing to work for low wages. They have also been criticized for having too many children. Even in modern politics, stereotypes about immigrants continue to be widespread.

| DISCUSSION STARTERS |

- What is your ethnicity? What is the history of your ethnicity in the United States? Were any of your ancestors immigrants?

- Why do you think immigrant groups are often treated as scapegoats for problems in society?

- Similar to Irish immigrants, Jewish immigrants were considered nonwhite when they arrived in the United States. Why might these immigrant groups have been viewed this way by society?

FEAR

AND

RACISM

The modern ideology of race in America was born with the colonial plantation system. Plantation owners sought to profit through slave labor, and the notion of race helped justify the inhumane treatment of these enslaved people. Defenders of such racism then used other factors, including religion, pseudoscience, and philosophy, to cement the idea of race. They helped turn race into a culturally accepted reality.

Another important factor also spurs these divisions between people. That force is fear. A feeling of insecurity can lead people to xenophobia and racism. During times of war or attacks on the country, many Americans have historically searched for ways to regain a sense of control. One way to do that is to blame a specific group of people. The enemy group is assigned negative attributes. They may be considered immoral, evil, or untrustworthy. Race helps the frightened people explain and justify such reactions. Entire groups of people are often prejudged and discriminated against. This can give the majority group a sense of control and power.

UNWELCOME ARRIVALS

In the 1860s, new policies in Japan focused on industrialization. By the 1890s, Japanese people who

An artist's depiction from the 1800s of Chinese immigrants working on the construction of the transcontinental railroad

lived in agricultural rural areas had limited chances for economic advancement. Many from the country made the journey to the United States in the late 1800s and early 1900s. They were hoping for new opportunities.

When they arrived, they found that a strong anti-Asian sentiment had been in place for decades. Chinese immigrants who had arrived in the western states found jobs in mining and in the railroad industry. As with many other poor immigrant groups, they were often willing to work for low wages. Racist reactions from working-class Americans erupted.

When Japanese immigrants arrived, labor unions, politicians, and white supremacists organized. They lobbied against the new arrivals. Legislation was passed to limit Japanese immigration. Other laws limited the amount of land the immigrants could buy. The government created separate schools for Asian children. In 1922, the US Supreme Court denied people born in Japan the opportunity to become US citizens.

THE IMMIGRATION ACT OF 1924

The Immigration Act of 1924 limited immigration to the United States. It lowered the yearly number of immigrants who could be admitted from any country. This was meant to limit immigration of southern and eastern Europeans. It also banned the immigration of Arabs and Asians.

JAPANESE INTERNMENT CAMPS

Japanese aircraft launched a surprise attack on the US naval base at Pearl Harbor, Hawaii, on December 7, 1941. The attack drew the United States into World War II (1939–1945). It also touched off a massive wave of anti-Japanese sentiment in America. On February 19, 1942, President Franklin D. Roosevelt issued Executive Order 9066. The order gave the government the ability to restrict certain groups of people from "military areas" designated by military officials.[1] To enforce the order, the US government removed and confined approximately 120,000 Japanese Americans who lived along the West Coast.[2] Most were

Japanese American internees found themselves under armed guard in the internment camps.

US citizens or legal residents. Large numbers of those who were removed were infants, school-age children, or young adults.

The United States was also at war with Germany. Some small groups of German Americans were interned, and others faced prejudice. Yet mass groups of German Americans were not interned.

Japanese Americans were treated like criminals. Many victims were jailed for up to four years. The camps were surrounded by barbed wire. The housing was substandard. The prisoners were not given adequate nutrition. They did not have proper health care. Internment destroyed their livelihoods. They lost their businesses, homes, and assets while being detained. Many suffered physically and psychologically. Several were killed by military guards for supposedly resisting orders.

THE JUSTIFICATION

Executive Order 9066 was issued as a supposed military necessity. It was designed to address Americans' fears about the Japanese attack. It was thought of as a protective measure to counter domestic spying and sabotage.

However, it was later documented that those who were incarcerated were not a threat. Not one Japanese American who was held had participated in spying. None of them had committed any act of sabotage. Many were upstanding, successful members of their communities. Some went on to show their loyalty to the United States despite their imprisonment. More than 30,000 Japanese Americans served in the military during the war, and more than 800 died in combat.[3] They distinguished themselves in battle. According to the Commission on Wartime Relocation and Internment of Civilians, a 1980 US government study, the causes for Japanese internment "were motivated largely by racial prejudice, wartime hysteria and a failure of political leadership."[5]

More than 40 years after the war, the US government admitted the Japanese internment camps were a mistake. Following pressure from leaders and advocates in the Japanese American community, Congress passed the Civil Liberties Act of 1988. It is often called the Japanese American Redress Bill. It acknowledged that "a grave injustice was done." It mandated a payment

ANTI-ASIAN SCAPEGOATING CONTINUES

In the summer of 1982, in a suburb of Detroit, Michigan, an automotive worker named Vincent Chin was the target of a hate crime. The attack was orchestrated by two angry laid-off automobile workers, a man named Ron Ebens and his stepson, Michael Nitz. They were told that their jobs were being eliminated due to the domination of Japan in the auto market. They mistakenly assumed that Chin, a Chinese American, was Japanese. They beat him to death with a baseball bat while he was out for a bachelor party with friends before his upcoming wedding.

The two men were charged with his death. They were found guilty of manslaughter. For killing Chin, they were punished with three years of probation and a fine of a few thousand dollars. Chin's death and the subsequent court ruling led to a movement for protected status for Asian Americans under civil rights laws.

of $20,000 in reparations to each victim.[6] Reparations were sent with a signed apology from the president of the United States on behalf of the American people.

XENOPHOBIA AFTER THE SEPTEMBER 11 ATTACKS

On September 11, 2001, terrorists belonging to the al-Qaeda terror network targeted the United States. A total of 19 terrorists hijacked four commercial jetliners. They flew two into the Twin Towers of the World Trade Center in New York City. They flew a third one into the Pentagon, the US military headquarters near Washington, DC. Passengers on the fourth plane struggled against the hijackers, and in the ensuing chaos the plane crashed in the Pennsylvania countryside. The attacks killed nearly 3,000 people.[7] Fear and anxiety became widespread in the country. Because the attackers were Muslim extremists, these feelings soon led to the targeting of Muslim Americans.

Islamophobia is an irrational fear and intense dislike of Muslims and the religion of Islam. Feelings of anger, suspicion, and contempt may stem from the belief that Muslims pose a threat to the United States. Perceptions of Muslims as the nation's enemies, along with a lack of knowledge about the religion of Islam, help foster Islamophobia.

People protested against Donald Trump when he called for a "total and complete shutdown of Muslims entering the United States" in a 2015 statement made during his presidential campaign.

These fears have led to systematic racial profiling. Law enforcement officers sometimes target people who look as though they could be Muslim or Arab. In a study of police officers in the midwestern United States, it was noted that some viewed Muslims as "foreigners."[8] They

ISIS is a militant group that uses terrorist tactics. Its goal is to set up an independent Islamic state in the Middle East. It tries to entice young male Muslims to join its fighting forces. This includes Muslims living in the United States.

According to a study on the dozens of Americans charged with ISIS–related crimes, most of them expressed dissatisfaction with life in the United States. American Muslims who felt rejected by anti-Muslim discrimination were more willing to support extremist groups. Anti-Muslim discrimination often becomes part of the recruiting efforts of ISIS and similar groups. Such groups play on fears that Western cultures have rejected Islam.

were perceived as a racial group. They were viewed as "un-American."[9] Many of the officers said they could determine who was Muslim based on skin color, hair color, or accent. Some police officers in the study stated that there was not a difference between Muslims and Arabs. Being Muslim, which is a religious affiliation, was not being separated from being Arab, which is an ethnicity. At the same time, many of the officers said they were interested in learning more about

Islam in order to better serve the Muslim members of their communities.

Islamophobia has become widespread in US culture. There have been anti-Muslim rallies, hate crimes, and threats made against Muslims throughout the United States. There are approximately 3.3 million Muslims living in the United States.[10] Only a few hundred have been accused of being involved in violent extremism. That means an overwhelming majority of Muslim Americans are ordinary, law-abiding citizens. Yet American Muslims have been harassed, beaten, and even murdered. Muslim children have been bullied, and Muslim women have been taunted. A Muslim congressman has received death threats. Several mosques have been vandalized.

Some politicians have spoken out against Islamophobia, hatred, and racism. But others have fueled these feelings. They frame US conflicts in the Middle East as being against Islam, rather than against a small minority of Islamic extremists.

| DISCUSSION STARTERS |

- Have you noticed examples of Islamophobia in the news over the last few years? Do these instances seem to be linked with fear?

- Do you feel an official government apology for past incidents, such as the Japanese internment, is a good idea?

- What are some ways in which people can fight fear-based racism?

WHY DOES RACISM PERSIST?

Racism has affected various ethnic and geographic groups from around the world. White, black, and brown people have all experienced racism throughout history. Why does racism persist? Will we ever be able to end it?

OBAMA ON RACE IN AMERICA

Racism remains a powerful force in the United States. Many people opposed to it, however, found hope in the election of President Barack Obama, the first African American president of the United States, in 2008. In a highly praised speech given during his presidential campaign, Obama spoke about race in US society:

I have asserted a firm conviction—a conviction rooted in my faith in God and my faith in the American people—that, working together, we can move beyond some of our old racial wounds, and that in fact we have no choice if we are to continue on the path of a more perfect union.[1]

FORMING GROUPS

For as long as humans have existed, they have had a tendency to form groups. A group typically acts to benefit those involved. Participants get something positive out of joining with their fellow group members.

Those in the group experience love or acceptance. Those outside the group may be subjected to rejection or hatred. The dividing lines between these groups are often arbitrary. Still, the lines can have real social consequences. Members of a group may assume they are smarter or more moral than those outside the group. Race, one of history's most powerful social constructs, is one of these artificial dividing lines.

Race as a scientifically defined physical attribute has been disproved by biologists and geneticists. Yet it has become such a pervasive cultural phenomenon that it has had significant, often damaging results. Race has become an ideology, a system of ideas and a particular way of thinking that shapes societies. However, the modern concept of race is a relatively recent invention. Just as it formed in response to historical circumstances, it could change again based on new developments.

TIME MAKES IT STICK

The ideology of race did not instantly spring into existence when the transatlantic slave trade began. It took time for

Black Lives Matter, which formed in the wake of sometimes-lethal discrimination against African Americans, is one of today's largest and most prominent antiracism movements.

it to be widely accepted. White Europeans may have long viewed Africans as significantly different from themselves, but the Europeans did not consider them a separate race of humanity. They did not regard them as naturally inferior.

Slave laws played a large part in making race an ideology. These laws drove policies and shaped people's beliefs. Once slave laws added the idea that the children of enslaved people were themselves slaves, the ideology of race was cemented. A person's race was linked to his or her natural state, and along with it came the attributes and qualities assigned to that race.

DISCRIMINATION AFTER SLAVERY

The passage of the Thirteenth Amendment to the US Constitution in 1865 ended slavery. Still, the American power structure continued to manipulate and dominate African Americans. Many former slaves could find only low-paying work in agriculture. Roads to new opportunities remained blocked. African Americans were denied access to education and professional training. Laws ensured they were still treated as second-class citizens.

Race can significantly affect a person's livelihood in America. Where people live, how well they are educated, their profession, and their overall health can be viewed along racial lines. A history of slavery and discrimination has resulted in whites having much higher levels of wealth than blacks on average. The median net worth

BUILD SOLIDARITY, TEAR DOWN RACISM

Activism and social movements can be effective in changing racial biases in society. The civil rights movement of the 1950s and 1960s brought about major changes in the United States. Today, activist groups such as Black Lives Matter are shedding light on racially charged violence. They are demanding change. Activists representing other groups are uniting behind the Black Lives Matter movement, hoping that solidarity will help strengthen their message and their cause.

Many Americans recognize that racism and prejudice are wrong. They may wonder what they can do to help bring about change. Experts suggest that learning about the history of groups outside of your own race, getting to know people outside of your own race, and recognizing biases in society are all important steps toward improving a person's understanding of race in America.

of households for whites is 16 times greater than that for blacks.[3] Whites are more likely to own a home as well. Many of these differences remain even when comparing at equal levels of education. Other statistics highlight racial disparities in the criminal justice system. Black men are six times as likely as white men to be incarcerated.[4]

NOW WHAT?

The ideology of race was created by people, but is it possible for people to undo it? Psychologists and activists argue one step toward fighting racism is to acknowledge that it exists. Those who claim that they are "color-blind" to race may think they are a part of the solution. The implication is that they don't judge others based on their skin tone. However, this viewpoint may not acknowledge the existing disparities in society between people of different races.

The idea of race is so deeply entrenched in modern American society that it may seem as though it has always existed. But studying the roots of racism shows that it is actually a relatively recent phenomenon. US history is filled with events and practices driven by racism. Slavery, Native American relocation, and Japanese internment were all closely linked to notions of race. Understanding how racism began, spread, and was maintained can help people recognize and fight against racism in the future.

| DISCUSSION STARTERS |

- What are some ways in which you could fight against racism personally?

- Do you think racism can be fully wiped out in the United States?

- Does the idea of race inevitably lead to racism, or can the two concepts exist separately?

ESSENTIAL FACTS

SIGNIFICANT EVENTS

- Christopher Columbus's voyage in 1492 led to widespread European colonization of the Americas and the colonial plantation system, which relied on slave labor.

- Slave codes from the late 1600s and early 1700s in the American colonies made race a legal reality. The laws gave power to white people and oppressed black people.

- President Franklin D. Roosevelt issued Executive Order 9066 on February 19, 1942. It led to the internment of 120,000 Japanese Americans based on their race.

- On September 11, 2001, the United States was targeted by terrorists who were Muslim. Fear-based Islamophobia spread in the wake of the attacks.

KEY PLAYERS

- Christopher Columbus, King Ferdinand, Queen Isabella, and Bartolomé de Las Casas were among the Europeans who spearheaded the colonization of the Americas and the establishment of slavery there.

- Philosophers and scientists of the 1700s and 1800s used their professions to promote racist ideologies, categorizing humans by race and typically placing whites at the top of artificial racial hierarchies.

- Andrew Jackson's Indian Removal Act forced the Cherokee people from their ancestral homes at gunpoint.

IMPACT ON SOCIETY

The concept of race is not scientifically valid, though the ideology of race has become a powerful force in American society. It has created a power hierarchy with whites at the top. Education, housing, income, and rates of incarceration are among the many indicators that are influenced by race. Historical events such as wars, mass immigration, and terrorist attacks have all triggered racist responses, deeply affecting US society.

QUOTE

"I have asserted a firm conviction—a conviction rooted in my faith in God and my faith in the American people—that, working together, we can move beyond some of our old racial wounds, and that in fact we have no choice if we are to continue on the path of a more perfect union."

—Barack Obama, March 18, 2008

GLOSSARY

ASSIMILATE
To adopt the ways of another culture.

CANNIBAL
A person who eats human flesh.

CONSTRUCT
An idea based on concepts that are grounded largely in opinions rather than facts.

DEMOGRAPHICS
Statistical data relating to the population as a whole, or to particular groups within it, showing factors such as race, average age, income, or education.

DNA
Deoxyribonucleic acid, the chemical that is the basis of genetics, through which various traits are passed from parent to child.

FRATERNITY

A feeling of friendship and mutual support.

HEATHEN

A person whose religion or customs are considered strange or uncivilized.

POPULIST

A member of a political party who states that he or she represents the common people.

PSEUDOSCIENCE

A system of theories, assumptions, and methods wrongly regarded as scientific.

SCAPEGOAT

A person who is unfairly blamed for something that others have done.

SERF

A farm laborer in the feudal system.

XENOPHOBIA

Fear or hatred of strangers or foreigners.

ADDITIONAL RESOURCES

SELECTED BIBLIOGRAPHY

Alexander, Michelle. *The New Jim Crow: Mass Incarceration in the Age of Colorblindness*. New York: New Press, 2012. Print.

Culotta, Elizabeth. "Roots of Racism." *Science* 336.6083 (2012): 825–827. Print.

Herbes-Sommers, Christine, dir. *Race: Power of an Illusion*. California Newsreel, Apr. 2003.

FURTHER READINGS

Burling, Alexis. *Race in the Criminal Justice System*. Minneapolis, MN: Abdo, 2018. Print.

Edwards, Sue Bradford. *What Are Race and Racism?* Minneapolis, MN: Abdo, 2018. Print.

Edwards, Sue Bradford, and Duchess Harris. *Black Lives Matter*. Minneapolis, MN: Abdo, 2016. Print.

WEBSITES

To learn more about Race in America, visit **abdobooklinks.com**. These links are routinely monitored and updated to provide the most current information available.

FOR MORE INFORMATION

For more information on this subject, contact or visit the following organizations:

THE ANTI-DEFAMATION LEAGUE
605 Third Avenue
New York, NY 10158
212-885-7700
http://www.adl.org/about-adl/

Originally founded in 1913 to fight anti-Semitism, the Anti-Defamation League is now a leading civil rights organization working to fight all forms of bigotry and defend democratic ideals and the civil rights of all people.

CAIR: COUNCIL ON AMERICAN-ISLAMIC RELATIONS
453 New Jersey Avenue, SE
Washington, DC 20003
202-488-8787
https://www.cair.com/about-us.html

The Council on American-Islamic Relations (CAIR) is a grassroots civil rights and advocacy group. CAIR is America's largest Muslim civil liberties organization.

SOUTHERN POVERTY LAW CENTER
400 Washington Avenue
Montgomery, AL 36104
334-956-8200
https://www.splcenter.org/

The Southern Poverty Law Center, formed in 1971, works to monitor hate groups and spread a message of tolerance to communities across the nation.

SOURCE NOTES

CHAPTER 1. JESSE OWENS BUSTS RECORDS AND MYTHS

1. "Race: The Power of an Illusion—Episode One." *California Newsreel.* California Newsreel, n.d. Web. 7 Feb. 2017.

2. Ibram X. Kendi. "On the Racist Ideas Jesse Owens Could Not Outrun." *Black Perspectives.* African American Intellectual History Society, 21 Feb. 2016. Web. 7 Feb. 2017.

3. "Race: The Power of an Illusion—Episode One." *California Newsreel.* California Newsreel, n.d. Web. 7 Feb. 2017.

4. Ibram X. Kendi. "On the Racist Ideas Jesse Owens Could Not Outrun." *Black Perspectives.* African American Intellectual History Society, 21 Feb. 2016. Web. 7 Feb. 2017.

5. Ibid.

6. "Race: The Power of an Illusion—Episode One." *California Newsreel.* California Newsreel, n.d. Web. 7 Feb. 2017.

CHAPTER 2. HUMAN DIVISIONS PRIOR TO RACE

1. "The Roots of Racism." *Rightsmatter.org.* Rightsmatter.org, 2006. Web. 7 Feb. 2017.

2. "Black Death." *Encyclopaedia Britannica.* Encyclopaedia Britannica, 6 Jan. 2017. Web. 7 Feb. 2017.

3. "The Roots of Racism." *Rightsmatter.org.* Rightsmatter.org, 2006. Web. 7 Feb. 2017.

CHAPTER 3. COLONIALISM, SLAVERY, AND RACE

1. John Noble Wilford. *The Mysterious History of Columbus.* New York: Knopf, 1991. Print. 96.

2. Lawrence A. Clayton. *Bartolome De Las Casas: A Biography.* New York: Cambridge, 2012. Print. 426.

3. "Spain's Slavery Contract." *Bristol and Transatlantic Slavery.* Discovering Bristol, n.d. Web. 7 Feb. 2017.

CHAPTER 4. EARLY SCHOOLS OF THOUGHT ON RACE

1. Justin E. H. Smith. "The Enlightenment's Race Problem and Ours." *New York Times*. New York Times, 10 Feb. 2013. Web. 7 Feb. 2017.

2. Ibid.

CHAPTER 5. SLAVERY IN THE COLONIES

1. "People and Events: The Virginia Slave Code." *Africans in America*. PBS, n.d. Web. 7 Feb. 2017.

2. "The Declaration of Independence." *America's Founding Documents*. National Archives, n.d. Web. 7 Feb. 2017.

3. "Thomas Jefferson, Notes on the State of Virginia." *The Founders' Constitution*. U of Chicago P, 2000. Web. 7 Feb. 2017.

CHAPTER 6. RACE AND NATIVE AMERICANS

1. "Race: The Power of an Illusion—Episode Two." *California Newsreel*. California Newsreel, n.d. Web. 7 Feb. 2017.

2. Donald M. Scott. "The Religious Origins of Manifest Destiny." *Divining America*. National Humanities Center, 2013. Web. 7 Feb. 2017.

3. "Racism: A History." *BBC Four*. BBC, 2010. Web. 7 Feb. 2017.

4. "Andrew Jackson: Fifth Annual Message." *American Presidency Project*. American Presidency Project, 2017. Web. 2 Feb. 2017.

5. "Trail of Tears." *Encyclopaedia Britannica*. Encyclopaedia Britannica, 18 Jan. 2017. Web. 7 Feb. 2017.

6. Ibid.

CHAPTER 7. RACE AND IMMIGRANTS

1. Gwen Sharp. "Stereotypes of the Irish." *Sociological Images*. Society Pages, 6 Oct. 2008. Web. 7 Feb. 2017.

2. Michael L. Krenn, ed. *Race and US Foreign Policy in the Ages of Territorial and Market Expansion, 1840 to 1900*. New York: Garland, 1998. Print. 45.

3. "The Texas Revolution: A Conflict of Cultures?" *Digital History*. U of Houston, 2016. Web. 8 Feb. 2017.

4. Simeon Ide. "The Conquest of California." 1880. Print. 128. Web. *Archive.org*. 23 Mar. 2017.

5. Jennifer Steinhauer, Jonathan Martin, and David M. Herszenhorn. "Paul Ryan Calls Donald Trump's Attack on Judge 'Racist,' but Still Backs Him." *New York Times*. New York Times, 7 June 2016. Web. 8 Feb. 2017.

CHAPTER 8. FEAR AND RACISM

1. "Transcript of Executive Order 9066." *Our Documents*. National Archives, n.d. Web. 8 Feb. 2017.

2. "Internment History." *Children of the Camps*. PBS, 1999. Web. 8 Feb. 2017.

3. John W. Traphagan. "Immigration, Racism, and the Internment of Japanese Americans." *Huffington Post*. Huffington Post, 21 Feb. 2016. Web. 8 Feb. 2017.

4. Rebecca K. Sharp. "How an Eagle Feels When His Wings Are Clipped and Caged." *Prologue Magazine*. National Archives, Winter 2009. Web. 8 Feb. 2017.

5. "Historical Documents." *Children of the Camps*. PBS, 1999. Web. 8 Feb. 2017.

6. "Internment History." *Children of the Camps*. PBS, 1999. Web. 8 Feb. 2017.

7. "9/11 Attacks." *History Channel*. History Channel, n.d. Web. 8 Feb. 2017.

8. Nour Abdelghani, Emily Dubosh, and Mixalis Poulakis. "Islamophobia and Law Enforcement in a Post 9/11 World." *University of Indianapolis Islamophobia Studies Journal* 3.1 (Fall 2015): 138–157. Print.

9. Ibid.

10. Besheer Mohamed. "A New Estimate of the US Muslim Population." *Fact Tank*. Pew Research Center, 6 Jan. 2016. Web. 8 Feb. 2017.

CHAPTER 9. WHY DOES RACISM PERSIST?

1. Barack Obama. "Transcript: Barack Obama's Speech on Race." *NPR*. NPR, 18 Mar. 2008. Web. 8 Feb. 2017.

2. Lindsey Cook. "US Education: Still Separate and Unequal." *US News and World Report*. US News and World Report, 28 Jan. 2015. Web. 8 Feb. 2017.

3. Laura Shin. "The Racial Wealth Gap: Why a Typical White Household Has 16 Times the Wealth of a Black One." *Forbes*. Forbes, 26 Mar. 2015. Web. 8 Feb. 2017.

4. George Gao. "Chart of the Week: The Black-White Gap in Incarceration Races." *Fact Tank*. Pew Research Center, 18 July 2014. Web. 8 Feb. 2017.

INDEX

ABOUT THE AUTHOR

Kelly Bakshi, MS Ed, is a nonfiction children's book author who writes about topics in social studies. She lives in Rye, New York, with her husband and two sons.